Fulfilled.
the journal

Healing | Health | Happiness

woodhall press

Woodhall Press, 81 Old Saugatuck Road, Norwalk, CT 06855
WoodhallPress.com

Cover design: Ammie Elliott
Layout artist: LJ Mucci

Library of Congress Cataloging-in-Publication Data available
ISBN 978-1-960456-04-5   (paper: alk paper)

First Edition
Distributed by Independent Publishers Group
(800) 888-4741

Printed in the United States of America

*This journal is dedicated to every single person
who has been a part of my story.*

*It's for all the perfectly imperfect people who are
trying to live their best life.*

*And to you, the beautiful person who has this journal in hand
and ready to become the most authentic version of yourself.*

*I also can't forget my Mom and brothers
(Thaddeous and Gregory). I have to mention them
specifically or I'll never hear the end of it. Ha!*

"

The pages of this journal are
intentionally quiet
so you have space to
speak your mind.

"

Fulfilled

Make The Pledge

I am beginning a life-changing journey.
This is my space to be present.
Vulnerable. Intentional. Truthful. Self-compassionate.
Forgiving, especially to myself.
And, to work through some things in order to embrace
the life that has been available to me all along.
This is my space to look inward so I can live happily from
the inside out.

This journal is for me.

Claim it. Write your name below.

Inhale.
Hold your breath.
Exhale.
Repeat.

Thank you for joining me here. It means you're ready to cut ties with what weighs heavily on your heart, heal wounds, nurture good health, and discover happiness!

Fulfilled

Living a fulfilled life — where life aligns with the reason you were born — is a tall order, but possible. It takes practice to live purposefully and passionately, and you'll have to push through the hard parts of your journey. (Hint: the hard parts help you to grow so you can thrive!)

Take a load off your mind, body, and spirit

This journal is designed to accompany my book, *Fulfilled. 52 Prescriptions for Healing, Health, and Happiness*, but certainly feel free to use it on its own. It is your safe space to be honest with yourself about your thoughts and feelings — about your life. With your pen (or pencil) pressed firmly, I hope you experience a cathartic emotional release and write (or doodle) your way to a beautiful life. You deserve it.

Sort out your story

Everyone has chapters in their story that need to be sorted out. Use this journal and it's inspirational quotes to work through it all. One small step at a time — through self-love, setting boundaries, forgiveness, choosing joy — you will dive deeper and open yourself to do more, be more, live more, and manifest more!

How to use this journal

Use this journal any way that transforms you into the dazzling person that only you can be. I created it to give you plenty of room to flesh out your thoughts on the Prescriptions in the accompanying book. Inspire reflection. Gain clarity. Practice positivity. Focus on the present. Face fears. Celebrate triumphs. I created it especially for you to get on with your life by releasing whatever makes you think you can't — because you can. Use this journal to breathe DEEPLY, process your TRUTH, and live BIGGER!

In harmony,

Dr. Bernadette

PS: I hope this journal breathes life into the person you were meant to be.

A positive attitude is the difference between attracting what you want, settling for what you get, or allowing your journey to totally devastate you.

_____ DATE

We are not in a
holding pattern in
our lives because
something is
missing, but
because we
haven't discerned
that whatever we
believe is missing
has been present
all along.

DATE _____

Instead of criticizing what makes you beautifully different, channel that
energy into loving who you are.

DATE _____

Tea Ritual

for practicing mindfulness

Write or doodle your thoughts
and feelings for each of
the following.

1. As you fill the vessel with
   water, **feel** the change of
   weight.

2. **Listen** to the sound of the
   boiling water.

3. As you pour the water
   onto the teabag, **watch** the
   color change.

4. **Notice** how the steam rises.

5. Pick up the mug and **feel**
   the gradient warmth.

6. **Smell** the aroma and note
   the different scents.

7. Move to take a seat and
   watch how the tea moves.

8. Take a sip, close your eyes,
   and savor the **taste**.

9. Open your eyes and slowly
   become aware of your
   surroundings and take note
   of what you **see**.

10. Repeat and enjoy.

DATE _____

Acceptance is not a vote
of approval, but rather
an end to a protest.
It acknowledges your
experience occurred
without interpreting what
happened, trying to fix it,
or judging your feelings
as being right or wrong.

DATE _____

Forgiveness is a very generous
gift to give to someone,
especially if they hurt you
deeply; however, they're
not the beneficiaries of
your forgiveness.

You are.

Letting bygones
be bygones, and
welcoming the
future in its' due
season is the
best way to quit
handing over
your chance to be
happy now.

_____ DATE

DATE _____

Hope is the heartbeat of
your best life. There's not
one single thing life can
throw at you that cannot
be defeated with hope.

DATE _____

DATE _____

The unhealed me treated peace like a cheap thrill; the healed me has
placed a high value on peace. All other things seem frivolous.

_____ DATE

DATE _____

We all have fears, but we don't have to live in fear. They don't have to run or ruin our lives, or make us feel like our hands are tied, because they're not.

Some of your
worst defeats
happen within
your own mind.
You don't stand
a chance against
negative thoughts
and self-ridicule.
It's an unfair fight.

A heart full of gratitude invites you to experience life's miracles every single day. It's not that you're wearing rose-colored glasses, you are simply choosing to focus on the roses rather than the thorns.

Breathing Ritual 1

for practicing feeling calm

Box Breathing

Imagine breathing around the sides of a box (or square). It slows down your breathing so it can return to its' normal rhythm. To give it a try:

1. Sit, stand, or lie down on your back.
2. Place a hand on the stomach and the other one on the chest.
3. Breathe in through your nose while slowly counting to 4.
4. Hold the breath for a count of 4.
5. Exhale for the count of 4.
6. Hold your breath again for a count of 4 without inhaling.
7. Keep going for 4 rounds.

Breathing Ritual 2

for practicing feeling calm

Humming Bee Breathing

Enjoy a soothing combination of breathing and vibrations. Here's how:

Find a quiet place.

Sit with your legs criss-crossed or in a chair.

Keep your face and jaw relaxed and lightly close your lips together.

Close both ears with the thumbs.

Rest the index and middle fingers over the eyes gently covering them.

Take a deep breath in through your nose.

Breathe out fully through your nose while making a humming sound.

Extend the breath for as long as it feels comfortable.

Continue for 5 breaths.

DATE _____

It's good that you do
not have to put a lot of
thought into breathing.
But if every now and then
you purposely think to
fully breathe, you could
not only change the
tempo of your breath, but
the tempo of your life.

DATE _____

> Believing in yourself does not mean being free of all doubts, it means moving forward with all-out-effort in spite of them.

You don't have
to travel to a
far-off exotic
place to take
time away from
preoccupying
thoughts and
busyness of life.
Anytime you
wish, simply
be still, retreat
from the world
around you, and
meditate.

Spiritual wellness
awakens a level of
consciousness which
serves as a moral
compass to live
authentically, aligned
with your purpose,
and at peace within
yourself.

DATE _____

DATE _____

A strong spiritual connection is to the soul as food is to the physical body, and as peace is to the mind. When spirituality takes center stage in your life, who you are meant to be becomes front and center.

_____ DATE

Prayer strengthens you to stand firm despite what the eyes see, the ears hear, and the mind thinks. It is the ultimate practice of positive thinking.

Your ducks won't
always be in row,
and a security net
won't always be
beneath you to
break your fall—
*take the leap
of faith.*

DATE _____

Laughter is a pressure-relief valve that helps you manage hard stuff
with a more positive mindset.

Transition Ritual

for practicing
work-life harmony

It's the end of your work day. Whether you work from home or commute, go to a private (or semi-private) place in your home that has no connection to work. If you live with others, let them know in advance that you have a transition routine to help unplug from work.

1. Light a candle or dim the lights to switch over your mindset.

2. While seated, think about any interactions you need to release. Are there projects, conversations, or tasks you need to put out of your thoughts?

3. Take note of any emotions, tension, or other sensations in your body.

4. Take a slow, deep breath.

5. Say aloud, "The workday is over and I did my best. I am home. I deserve to be present."

6. Take another slow, deep breath.

7. Stand and notice the weight of your feet against the floor. Sense the connection.

8. Head to your bedroom and limit interactions with others.

9. Change into more comfortable clothes.

10. Return to your quiet space and do a body scan.

Body Scan Ritual

for practicing connection with yourself

1. Lie on your back with your arms at your side. Casually look around and note that you are safe.

2. Close your eyes and bring your attention to how your body feels against the floor.

3. Take a slow, deep breath and listen to your slow exhale. Do this two more times.

4. Gradually shift your focus back to your body.

5. Move your attention to your feet. How do they feel? Heavy? Achy? Fine?

6. From your feet, slowly scan up your body, in rhythm with your breathing. Do you have tightness, pressure, pain, or other sensations?

7. As you scan upwards, breathe deeply and soften any tense muscles.

8. When you reach your head, notice your jaw. If it's clenched or tight, let it fall loose.

9. Continue to the crown of your head.

10. Take a longer, deeper breath. As you exhale, shift your attention to your whole body.

11. When you're ready, open your eyes.

DATE _____

Setting boundaries is the
courage to trust yourself
to honor and think of
your own wellbeing, *first*.

_____ DATE

Subconscious breathing keeps you
physically alive, and conscious
breathing is the oxygen that
unites your mind, body, and spirit
so you can be more

present to live.

_____ DATE

Healthy
boundaries are
not intended to
be unkind, but to
establish ground
rules so you
don't disappoint
yourself by
trying not to
disappoint others.

_____ DATE

DATE _____

Choosing joy does not mean
living in denial. It's accepting
life as it is without trying to
force it to be anything different.
Joy doesn't always make perfect
sense; but neither does life.

DATE _____

_____ DATE

DATE _____

The freedom to show up as the person you were created to be
is its own reward.

Self-love is the best love story you'll ever live.